A Father's Guide to Raising Daughters

Will Kenlaw

Printed in Victoria, Canada

National Library of Canada Cataloguing in Publication Data

Kenlaw, Will, 1959-
    A father's guide to raising daughters : because I
need one! / Will Kenlaw.
Includes bibliographical references.
ISBN 1-4120-0129-3
    1. Fathers and daughters. 2. Parenting. 3. Child
rearing. I. Title.
HQ755.85.S6 2003   649'.133   C2003-901930-6

TRAFFORD

This book was published *on-demand* in cooperation with Trafford Publishing.
On-demand publishing is a unique process and service of making a book available for retail sale to the public taking advantage of on-demand manufacturing and Internet marketing. **On-demand publishing** includes promotions, retail sales, manufacturing, order fulfilment, accounting and collecting royalties on behalf of the author.

Suite 6E, 2333 Government St., Victoria, B.C. V8T 4P4, CANADA
Phone   250-383-6864   Toll-free   1-888-232-4444 (Canada & US)
Fax   250-383-6804   E-mail   sales@trafford.com
Web site   www.trafford.com   TRAFFORD PUBLISHING IS A DIVISION OF TRAFFORD
HOLDINGS LTD.
Trafford Catalogue #03-0497   www.trafford.com/robots/03-0497.html

10   9   8   7   6   5   4   3   2

Introduction

Necessity is the Mother of Invention

I am the father of four daughters and the husband of one wife. I wrote this book because *I needed it* and couldn't find it. Due to a seven-year gap between my first and second daughters, I have a difficult time remembering all the teaching, events, and activities done with my first daughter.

It suddenly struck me, "I have to do all these things over again, three more times!   I can't remember all the good stuff we did, all the great conversations we had, etc." I need a roadmap or guidebook so that I can give the same "quality of interaction" with my youngest three daughters as I did with "number one."

I asked the question, "Does a guidebook or roadmap exist?" I couldn't find one.

Since "necessity is the mother of invention," I decided to write down as much as I could remember from the first 14 years with my oldest daughter, for use with my younger daughters. Then the thought hit me, "Can't other men benefit from this? If 'somebody' wrote a book then all men could benefit." Will "Somebody" write this book so that I will have the information and knowledge to successfully raise daughters? I couldn't wait for "Somebody," so I wrote it. I hope it helps you and your daughters.

"Build a snowman with her and create a memory that will last forever."

Dedication

This book is dedicated to Sissy, Dach, Bone, and Fe (my four daughters). You are truly my treasures from heaven, my blessings from an all knowing, all wise, all loving God. He knew I needed girls, even when I didn't. You are more precious than rubies, more valuable than gold. I wouldn't trade any of you for ten sons. Kristin (14), Rachel (7), Grace(4), and Faith(2). Some of the greatest questions came from you: "Daddy, what is time? Daddy, why do you have to work? Daddy, where is God?"

Table of Contents

1. Tell her you love her <u>every day</u>

Nothing else in this book is more important. **You can do everything else in this book and fail, if she doesn't know unequivocally and unconditionally that you love her.** I say I love you to my daughters each day when I drop them off to school and each night after I tuck them into bed.

I credit my wife with instilling this habit in me. During our third year of marriage we had a long discussion about "PDAs," public displays of affection. She wanted to hear "I love you" more often than I wanted to say it. Her most convincing argument was, "what happens if when we separate during the day, one of us dies, and that was the last opportunity to say "I love you," and it wasn't said for fear of embarrassment.

"How would you feel? Would you say it if given a second chance? Then say it on every first chance!"

I couldn't defeat that argument and thank God I couldn't. It has made our relationship stronger and more loving. My wife used the same argument for kissing each time we separate during the day, and when we come back together. As our daughters have grown, they picked up on it right away. They expect a kiss from daddy whenever I leave them during the day, and to hear the words, "I love you." They will follow me to the door if I forget, and the little ones will sometimes cry if I go outside the house before kissing them.

2. Pray Over Her Every Night

Cover her in the blood of Jesus for protection daily; bind and rebuke any unclean spirits; pray for sweet dreams and no nightmares; pray for excellent health; pray for prosperity in all she touches; pray for her success in school; pray for her to be a blessing to others; pray for her to be God's instrument in a dead and dying world; **pray for a God Fearing, Holy Spirit Filled Husband to be her partner and best friend.**

Teach her about God: Father, Son, and Holy Spirit. He is triune and yet one. Teach her that God the Father is: omnipotent, omniscient, righteous, holy, awesome, and eternal. Teach her that God the Son is: incarnate, flesh and spirit, all man and all God, our redeemer, our savior, our mediator, and our example. Teach her that

God the Holy Spirit is: sent by the Son, our power on Earth, our counselor, our helper, our teacher, the bestower of Gifts, and the revealer of hearts.

Teach her to Pray

Night Prayer

Now I lay me down to sleep,
I pray the Lord my soul to keep.
If I should die before I wake,
I pray the Lord my soul to take.
God Bless Daddy, Mommy, (brothers and sisters'
names),
And all my friends and loved ones,
In sweet Jesus name I pray,
Amen.

Morning Prayer

Now I pick me up to go,
I pray the Lord my soul to know.
If I should die before I sleep,
I pray the Lord my soul to keep.
God Bless Daddy, Mommy, (brothers and sisters'
names),
And all my friends and loved ones,
In sweet Jesus name I pray,
Amen.

3. Teach her about money: *"It doesn't come from ATMs."*

Teach her that money is a tool. It must be understood and managed. **It must be mastered or it will master her**. Teach her about giving, especially tithes and offerings, to her place of worship. Teach her that it is more blessed to give than to receive, and that the good she does for others will return to her.

Also teach her about savings and investing. My second daughter, Rachel (7), doesn't understand the big deal about money. She says, "Just go to the ATM and get some more." The funny thing is, my father made the money, but my mother <u>taught me</u> about money. She took me to the bank to open a savings account. She took me to the telephone company and showed me how to pay bills. She showed me what a checkbook was and how to use it. Explain budgets, spending, short-term savings, and long-term savings to your daughter.

Our girls receive a weekly allowance when they become 6 years old. It's a dollar. From that dollar, they give 10 cents to God as a tithe. They give 10 cents as an offering. They must save at least 30 cents in "long-term" savings (until Christmas, for a large purchase, or indefinitely). They can spend 50 cents whatever way they desire. The allowance increases one dollar per year. Our fourteen year old receives a nine-dollar allowance.

The allowance is designed to teach them about money: how to earn it, save it, spend it, and give it. The allowance is tied to weekly chores. If the chores are "intentionally" not performed, then no allowance is given. No work, no pay. The allowance also teaches the child to count money: the different coins, the different dollar denominations, dividing money into different categories (tithes & offerings for Church, savings, spending money).

Our girls know that we have a budget. As a matter of fact, when they want something that's not in the budget, the request usually ends in a chorus of, "We know! We know! It's NOT in the budget!!!"

4. Teach her about boys: *"They are hunters, don't become prey."*

Teach your daughter NOT to become a notch on some male's belt or headboard. Boys in all cultures are conditioned and socialized to be "hunters." Find it, kill it or subdue it, bring it home, go do it again tomorrow. Girls in all cultures are conditioned and socialized to be "nurturers." Conceptualize it, incubate it, birth it, teach it, develop it, do it again. Boys in American culture are conditioned to be promiscuous and aggressive, e.g. the Old Spice Man, James Bond, and SuperFly. Girls in American culture are conditioned to be virtuous and beautiful, e.g. Betsy Ross, Miss America, and Barbie.

Even 30 years of feminist propaganda and equal rights momentum have not significantly changed the afore mentioned norms. Let's be real. Only parental influence can significantly change or reinforce these norms. We as fathers must decide if we are going to teach our daughters to be mothers, mothers/astronauts, or just astronauts. Regardless of the choice, we as fathers make, **we must teach our daughters about boys**. And it's more than just, "Boys only want one thing." It's: 1) guard your heart, 2) understand the "game," 3) follow your values not your feelings, 4) stand for something or fall for everything (smooth lines, handsome faces, great bodies, "good" hair☺).

5. Teach her about sex: *"It's a gift from God, that Satan works to pervert."*

You must discuss: sex as a gender (males and females), sex the physical act, and the types of sex. That's right, the types of sex. Don't kid yourself. When my oldest daughter was five or six, she asked, "What is oral sex?" One of her classmates mentioned it to her and she (thank God!) decided to ask Daddy and Mommy for an explanation. Don't rush any of these discussions. Don't feel as though once you've started, then you must discuss every topic or detail. **Let her age, maturity, and questions guide your discussion points and depth of detail.** Give her what she needs to know to "drive defensively" on the sexual highway. Inform her so she's not "gullible Gertrude" among her peers.

entertainment. Teach your daughter not to be the "entertainment" for a young man's fancy. **Teach her to pursue "love" with a level head, a moral heart, and a clean body.**

"Love" desires to commit, wants to commit, and wants an "exclusive" relationship. Anyone that tells her differently is NOT describing "love." They may be describing lust or selfishness, but not "love."

7. Her first date should be with YOU

Schedule Monthly Dates with your daughter, starting <u>no later than</u> 13 years old. **If you want her to marry a gentleman, then <u>be</u> one**. When you take her on dates, open the car door for her, pull out her chair for her, etc.

The initiation of dating is the "dread" of every father. We all start out the same way, "She's not dating until she's 30." Most of us realize that if we wait that late, then our daughters will have no experience, and worse, no experience guided by our wisdom. No experience and no wisdom means, "she's meat on a stick" to any guy with a smooth line and the ability to show her attention.

The other great misery of fathers is the contradiction between "dating" and "courting."

person. If you are bold and courageous, she will see God as bold and courageous, and desire to be a bold and courageous person. And the one that comes up with every single daughter----fairness. If you are fair, she will see God as fair, and desire to be a fair person.

One of a father's toughest teaching assignments is to teach daughters that "life is NOT fair." (See Chapter 18) That's one of the primary reasons for courage. They will be mistreated, cheated, defrauded, and manipulated, but they must have the courage to "fight the good fight," stand up to evil, and do the right thing even if no one else will.

9. Perseverance & Persistence

It takes 3 years to become good at anything. I started telling my oldest daughter, Kristin, this when she started karate at 8 years old. Early on she wanted to quit. The "forms" were too hard. A "form" is a specific sequence of punches, blocks, and kicks which must be memorized and demonstrated to instructors and judges. We added private, one-on-one lessons to supplement her group lessons. She did Karate for 3 ½ years earning the yellow, red, green, blue, purple, and brown belts. All these accomplishments from a kid who initially wanted to quit in the first month.

When she discovered it would probably take her another 3 years to get the black belt (her karate school doesn't award black belts often to anyone under 16), she decided to expand her interests and took up basketball and tennis. Again, I have to remind her (about once per month during the season) that it takes about 3 years to become "good" at anything. Why 3 years? The first year, you learn the rules. The second year, you get your own rhythm and begin experimenting. The third year, you flow and are more relaxed in your own skills and confidence, and you begin push yourself beyond your capabilities.

My second daughter, Rachel, is now 7 years old and taking karate. She wants to quit because "it's boring." Translation: I haven't learned the forms or earned a belt, hence no excitement. So once again, I'm teaching her, "It takes 3 years to become proficient (good) at anything." And you must practice daily to become good. Her older sister overcame the same self-created objection by practicing 5 days a week and taking private lessons to improve. Rachel needs to practice daily, but hasn't quite developed the discipline at seven years old. She also may not have the attention span for karate. She is a very different child than her older sister.

Although this book is written to help you remember the things done with older daughters, each child is unique. While you can do the same activities, they will not yield identical outcomes. The important point is to provide a comparable number and type of experiences for each daughter. Create as many memories as possible with each child. *Have as many teaching moments as you can with each one.*

10. Pressure: *Rise to the Challenge*

I picked up my 14 year old from basketball practice this week. As we rode home in the car she began to cry. I asked why. She said the coach was constantly riding her, correcting her, focusing on her throughout the practice session. Through her tears, she whined, "Why can't we have a junior varsity? I don't want to be on varsity. Last year, other schools had ninth and tenth graders on their middle school team. Why can't our school do the same?"

I reminded her that it is a blessing to be able to play varsity in the ninth grade. Her grandmother had played varsity in the ninth through twelfth grades, and had been a starter every year. "But things were different then!"

"You're right," I said, "but freshmen were still singled out, had to make the big adjustment from middle school ball to the varsity level, and coaches were tougher at the varsity level. Maybe today was just your day. Maybe the coach picks a different person each practice to focus on teaching, correcting, improving. A certain amount of this, you're just going to have to <u>suck up</u>."

There's a reason why **80% of female business executives have played varsity sports**. I think this is it. They learn how to deal with pressure. They learn how to rise to the occasion. They learn how to perform, when others fold.

I told my oldest daughter about a movie her mother and I had watched called "Love and Basketball". When the central character in that movie moved from high school to college, she too complained that the coach hated her, singled her out to ride. But one day she met with the coach to ask why.

The coach explained that those who had the most potential, were the ones she rode the hardest. The coach warned her to start worrying when she didn't correct her, push her, or criticize her. When the senior guard on her college team went down with an injury, the freshman was asked to start in her place. She rose to the challenge and kept the starting role even after the senior healed from her injuries.

Two days later, I asked my daughter how practices were going. She smiled and said, "… very well. We're starting to bond as a team. The upper class girls are starting to talk to us and help us."

My high school's varsity basketball coach
gave his players a poem to memorize. One of the
players had to recite it after every practice
session. Its purpose was to teach the players to
never surrender and never give up. The poem
is called, "Don't Quit." Its writer is anonymous.
I dedicate it to another coach, the father of one of
my best friends.

**The following poem is dedicated to the
Life and Legacy of Coach Kenny Owens.**

DON'T QUIT

When things go wrong, as they sometimes will,
When the road you're trudging seems all uphill,
When the funds are low and the debts are high,
And you want to smile, but you have to sigh,
When care is pressing you down a bit-----
Rest if you must, but don't quit.

Life is queer with it twists and turns,
As every one of us sometimes learns,
And many a fellow turns about
When he might have won had he stuck it out.
Don't give up though the pace seems slow----
You may succeed with another blow.

Often the goal is nearer than
It seems to a faint and faltering man;
Often the struggler has given up
When he might have captured the victor's cup;
And he learned too late when the night came down,
How close he was to the golden crown.

Success is failure turned inside out----
The silver tint of the clouds of doubt,
And you never can tell how close you are,
It may be near when it seems afar;
So stick to the fight when you're hardest hit----
It's when things seem worst that you mustn't quit.

TAKE IT EASY, MY FRIEND.....WE NEED YOU!

11. Discipline with Love

Spank when she defies your authority. Never spank when you're angry. Never spank to prove you're more powerful. Some people say never spank. The following example explains one reason for its necessity.

You and your daughter are walking together on the sidewalk of a busy downtown street. Across the street, your daughter sees a cotton candy vendor wagon. She breaks the grip from your hand and runs toward the traffic in the street. She is on a mission to get to the cotton candy vendor. If she ever starts running into a busy traffic intersection, she needs to have learned to respect your authority verbally without question. It could save her life.

Spanking teaches respect for authority. It teaches a child that there are limits in some areas of life. It also teaches the importance of obedience.

Spanking is very hard for a father of a daughter or daughters. From the time she is born, you live to see her smile. **"Daughters are given by God to warm a father's heart."**

When my first-born was under 12 months old, I would do almost anything to keep her from crying or stop her crying. It just hurt my heart to hear her cry. It took time, but I learned that crying is not always a bad thing. She was 14 months old the first time I spanked her, a tap on the leg to stop her defiant behavior. She was stunned. I could see it in her eyes-----"my Daddy spanked me!" Mommy had spanked her long before that day. But Daddy was a different matter. He was the one she had wrapped around her little finger. He was the one who jumped when she said "Boo!" She knew her power at 14 months old.

Spanking is about discipline and getting her attention. It's not about power or inflicting hurt. A typical spank might use 1 to 5 percent of the muscular power an adult could use. It's not about power or inflicting hurt. It's about getting the child's attention and focusing her on the teaching you're trying to convey.

It's amazing how much more attentive a child becomes just with the mention of spanking. My wife and I are complimented wherever we go on how respectful, well mannered, and attentive our children are. It's no accident or coincidence. It is taught, and spanking is a part of that teaching. Dr. Spock must **not** have had children. Defiance is born. Discipline is learned.

12. Bond with her Early

I didn't realize how much I had bonded with my children until our third daughter (Grace) came.

I was tremendously busy as a business executive at the IBM Corporation. I lived in Maryland but worked 3 to 5 days a week in New York City. That meant living away from my family in hotels two to four nights a week.

My third daughter, Grace, was born during this period. By my third year of doing this, I noted that one of my girls (or my wife) would cry each week as I left for the airport. It weighed on me, but not heavily enough to give up the climb up the executive ladder.

One day I was talking with Grace and I realized that she was unusually shy towards me. She is a shy child, but this was still odd. When I asked her mother about it, I received an answer I hadn't expected----"She doesn't <u>know</u> you."   I was dumbfounded.   "What do you mean she doesn't know me?"

Let's see, I'm only gone four days a week. And when I'm in town, I usually spend Saturday and Sunday doing Church work.   Yikes! Maybe she's right.   My baby doesn't know me.   But I was busy like this when Rachel (#2) was born. Wasn't I?   I was, but I didn't spend as many nights on the road.   And I had **bonded** with her. How?

After some soul searching, I discovered that I usually bonded with the girls during a time when they were sick----a cold, the flu, diarrhea, something that forced me to hold her in my arms for hours, perhaps all night.   Colic in our first-born forced me to sing to her for two hours every

13.   Teach her about beauty

"Beauty is only skin deep but ugly goes clear to the bone!" That's the common belief, but there's much more to be discussed with our daughters. Don't let TV, magazines, and Barbie Dolls define what's beautiful and what's not in her life. When an Asian American wants blond hair because she's convinced this is the standard of beauty to which to aspire, then her father failed to teach her true beauty.

Daughters are beautiful to their fathers... forever. However, she will realize this by the time she becomes a teenager and will no longer accept your standard answer, "of course I think you're beautiful. You're the most beautiful little girl on the planet."

Discuss with her, outer beauty and inner beauty. Discuss standards of beauty and who sets them. Discuss Barbie Doll beauty and Miss American beauty. Discuss Caucasian beauty, Asian beauty, African American beauty, Indian beauty, and whatever ethnic group you belong to. Discuss "eye of the beholder" beauty. Discuss beauty from God's point of view.

Discuss "true" beauty. It comes from love: love of one's self, love of God, and love from family and friends. Discuss beauty in the real world context----attractive people get advantages, but it doesn't change the content of their character.

Beauty is number 13 for a reason. It's a weird one. To your daughter it's probably second in importance, second only to telling her you love her unconditionally.

Too many girls grow up with a distorted view of true beauty.   Too many girls grow up with low self-esteem and a poor self-image due to "cultural and social brainwashing" on beauty. Don't let it happen to your little girl. **She is the most beautiful little girl on the planet**.

Tell her millions of men will think so. How do you know? There are three <u>billion</u> males on the planet. Tens of millions will think she's beautiful. Millions will think she's gorgeous …..and they are right. She is!

14. Discuss her menstrual cycle with her.

It doesn't mean she's now a "woman," but it does mean she's on her way to becoming one.

Her cycle is a gift from God. It means God has given her the ability to sustain and nurture life. Half the population (men) on Earth does NOT possess this gift, nor do one out of six women in the United States. It is truly a gift, a blessing. Her menstrual cycle is a personal responsibility. It is the precursor to exponential development: emotionally, mentally, physically, and psychologically. She should never be ashamed of it or make excuses for it.

15. "Hoochie" Mama Clothes

"Dad, do you think I'm going to dress that your way once I leave for college?" These are the words of my fourteen year-old. "At that point it will be your choice. Until then, you will be instructed on how to dress properly and modestly. That's my job....to teach you the correct way to dress."

How many fathers have had this exchange with their teenage daughters? It's either showing cleavage or pants so tight they look painted on. "You don't need to wear clothes so tight that anyone can see every curve of your body. Those pants are so tight, I can see your pimples and birthmarks!" My daughter could only laugh at that pronouncement.

A father's great challenge is to teach his daughter to see herself from the eyes of a male. Initially, daughters are clueless in this regard. Later, they become "conveniently ignorant." After learning the affect they can have on teenage boys, or males in general, they sometimes like the "power." (A "Hoochie Mama"--- a scantily or provocatively dressed female--- <u>loves</u> the power.)

Like so many teenagers, my fourteen year old is dying to be fifteen. She feels that dressing according to the latest styles, i.e. what peers are wearing, is essential to maintaining her social standing. The problem is that peers are wearing V-neck blouses, hip hugging and crotch clinging pants, spaghetti straps, see-through fabrics, and body piercings.

So here's the discussion a father must have with his daughter.

Father: "The way you dress reflects your values, your self-esteem, and your tastes. If you are driven primarily by what other people say or do, then you are no more than a puppet or manikin."

Daughter: "Why do other parents let their daughters wear anything they want?"

Father: "Maybe they don't care, or they wear similar nonsense. Hence they think it's cute."

Daughter: "Why do I have to have over-protective parents?"

Father: "Because God loves you. Because we are preparing you for greatness."

Daughter: "But your thinking reflects the old days, not today."

Father: "Darling, there's nothing new under the sun. At the turn of the century, it was scandalous for women to show their ankles in the latest new dresses. In the 1920s, it was shameful for women to show their calves. In the 1940s, fishnet stockings and hosiery with dark seams drawing attention to their legs was the rage. In the 1960s, it was miniskirts. In the 1970s it was tube tops and hip hugger pants. All these so-called 'hip' clothes keep recycling themselves with each new generation. What you're going through isn't new. How 'you' deal with it is."

Daughter: "What? Do you think some boy or man is going to attack me based on what I wear?"
Father: "You would be surprised. 'Hoochie Mama' clothes tell males that: 1) this girl *'wants'* to be looked at, 2) this girl *'wants'* to be talked to or engaged, and 3) some guys way over read it to mean, 'she wants me to take her.' Don't be naïve. We live in a society that conditions males to be attackers and to 'sow their wild oats.' Both are immoral and wrong, but that's our reality. That's what you have to navigate through."

16.   Teach her about Politics

What are republicans (I've got mine, you get yours), democrats (I've got mine, maybe I'll help you get yours), independents (I've got mine, I hope you get yours), and little "green" men (I've got mine, everything is to be shared anyway).

We live in an age of democracy in most of the Western Hemisphere, dictatorships, pseudo-democracy, and communism in most of the Eastern Hemisphere, and socialism sprinkled about in each hemisphere. Our daughters need to know these concepts.

We live in an age of Saddam Hussein and North Korean dictators, an age where every country wants "nuclear" weapons and power, but none know how to use them responsibly.

The most important politics are local. Teach your daughter to understand city and county politics, the power structures, and the various constituencies. Teach her to map that against state and national politics. And lastly, **teach her to think globally, internationally.**

17.   Ask her how she "feels" and what she "thinks"

Ask her how she "feels" and what she "thinks" rather than questions requiring "Yes" or "No" answers. She wants to talk more than you know, maybe more than you want to listen. But listening is easy and..... cheap.

Talk to her! Have deliberate, protracted conversations with her. Start early and continue them when she's a teenager (i.e. gray hair producer). I suspect for most men, this will be harder than it sounds. For me it is, because I'm not a proactive talker. I'm more introvert than extrovert. It must be overcome.

Women talk to establish and build relationships. Men talk to get answers. Like most men, it's difficult for me to talk just for the sake of talking. But that's exactly what I'm recommending to fathers with their daughters. Talk to her!

Ask her open-ended questions, which require elaboration on her part. Then ask her how she "feels about that." Then ask for her thinking, her logic, her rationale, and her justification. Ask questions that allow her to talk. And listen! Stay engaged in the conversation. Use body language and expressions that show your engagement ("Oh! Ah! Okay! Then what? Why?")

There will come a time in your relationship when you will need her to spill her guts to you, in order for you to help her. Without these types of conversations in advance, you won't have the foundation and trust for her to openly talk to you.

18. Teach her Life's NOT fair

That's a reality of life she will learn early and often. Prepare her to deal with it positively and constructively. Tell her, **"Fairness was lost when the Garden of Eden was closed until further notice."**

It's not fair that she will never get to meet her grandmother who died before she was born. It's not fair that women are treated unequally in most societies on this planet. It's not fair that rich women get richer, while poor women seem to get poorer. It's not fair that girls who develop faster physically, get more attention from boys than those who are slower to develop.

Who ever told her life was fair? Ask her. I'm convinced that the notion came to her from fairy tales. Cinderella always marries the prince.

Sleeping Beauty is always awakened by the kiss of a handsome prince. The ugly duckling learns that it is really a beautiful swan. Therefore, when a girl's happy ending fails to materialize, "Life isn't fair!!!"

The best answer I give to my daughters came from my Church Pastor. *"This is not the world that God made. This is the world which turned its back on God."*

The world that God made "was fair." It was perfect. It was Eden. Disobedience and sin broke and destroyed that perfection. Fairness was lost then. Individual men and women work hard to restore fairness, but it is never a constant. It's something that must be fought for, worked for, and clung to.

19.   Give her inheritance early and often

Pass along the family's best wisdom.
She doesn't have to wait for Confucius or Henry David Thoreau.   Grammy, Papa, Uncle Boot, and others, have lots to share with the babies. Capture that wisdom and pass it on to your daughter.   The following is an example from our family.

KENLAW FAMILY WISDOM

1. God is above all, over all, under all, is ALL.......The Holy Bible

2. Never forget where you came from............"Grand Ma Hattie"

3. A man's got to do what a man's got to do......."Grandpa Will"

4. Get your education, they can never take that away..."Papa" Randolph Ore

5. Your moccasins will outlast your money...........the Indian blood in us.

6. There is greatness within you................Uncle Boot

7. It takes 3 Years to become the "expert" at anything, be patient, work hard... "Dad"

8. Attitude is Everything!!!

9. Stand Up For What's Right, Even If You Stand Alone.

10. The Little Voice That Warns You **IS** God!

11. Love is more important than money.

12. Money is important, but only a tool to be a blessing to family, Church, and others.

Create Your Own _____ Family Wisdom

(Your Name)

1.
2.
3.
4.
5.
6.
7.
8.
9.
10.
11.
12.

20.   Ages Prenatal to 18 months: *Spoil her*

Love her to pieces! If there's got to be some period in which to spoil her, then this is likely the lowest risk period. She will learn about the loving arms of God, from the loving arms of her earthly father----YOU.   During the first 3 months she will learn your voice. By six months she will learn your face and your voice. **She will be "hooked" on you, and you will be hooked on her.**

Cherish this time. It is good enough to melt in your mouth. Words cannot describe it adequately.

21.   Ages Prenatal to 8 years:
Read to her

The Bible and children's books are best, but
it really doesn't matter, as long as it's age
appropriate. She loves stories and she loves
hearing your voice. I'm working harder to read to
my two, four, and seven year-olds, 15 minutes
before bedtime.

My four year-old actually sacrificed dessert
in order to not be late for story time. That
reminded me of just how important it is to read to
her. She loves it. She will also develop a love for
reading.

We must have read everything to our oldest
child. We read the Bible, children's books,
magazines, newspapers, job reports, Sunday
School lessons, Bible study lessons, etc. By the
time she was ready for sixth grade, she had read

close to 200 books on her own. She reads in the car. She reads with a flashlight in her bed. She loves to read. *Read to your daughter.*

One of the greatest determinants for success in elementary school, and school in general, is the ability and love for reading. If your daughter develops a love for reading, and you nurture it, she will not have academic problems in school. She may have challenges, like maintaining straight A's, but she will not be hampered by the basics of reading, comprehension, and test taking.

Our seven year-old is following the same path. At six she began to read independently of us parents. We suddenly realized that we needed to get some books on the shelves for her. I went to the garage and basement, and dug out 30 to 50 of the books our oldest had read, when she was

7 to10 years old. Now the seven year-old likes to read in the car and on the top bunk of her bunk beds. She gets a great sense of accomplishment from finishing a book.

22.　Ages 18 months to 4 years: *Give her "her up"*

Pick her <u>up</u> into your arms whenever she asks you to. My oldest daughter would say, "I need my up." Or, " Uppy please." Or, "Daddy, up. Daddy up." I would pick her up and say, "What is it sweetie?" The "it" was usually just being in my arms. My two year-old now says it, and it's just as precious now as it was the first time I heard it 13 years ago.

For about two months after writing this, each of my daughters began asking me to pick them up. It was a challenge to test if I would be true to what I'm writing to you. Each time one asked, I remembered what I wrote, **"Give her 'her up'."** And I did.

23.   Ages 4 years to 6 years: *Tuck Her In*

As often as possible, tuck her into bed. Teach her prayers and listen while she prays. My oldest asked me to do this until she was a teenager, and sometimes still asks.

Bedtime is a uniquely special moment each day. It's a time when all of life for your daughter slows to a sudden pause. Little children often resist this pause. They want to always be "going." The time is special because it's like a timeout, but with "positive" attention from the parent. It's precious one-on-one time. "How was your day? How do you feel? Is anything bothering you? Why were you so cranky today? How's your cold? Do you feel better now? Are you ready for a peaceful night of rest? Are you ready for sweet dreams?"

It's a special time to kiss your daughter. It's a special time to hug your daughter. It's a time to show her your love as the last thing she sees before unconsciousness. She goes to sleep with your love on her mind and in her heart.

At five years old, I gave her a music box. It was very ornate, yet inexpensive, with a beautiful tune---a little treasure. She truly treasures it as a special memory. When I recently mentioned that it was time for me to buy a similar music box for one of her sisters, the oldest daughter expressed her displeasure with that idea. Her mother admonished her----"Your sisters deserve to have the same special gifts and memories with their father as you have had." That's one of the primary purposes of this book.

24. Ages 6 to 8: *Teach her to ride a bicycle*

Bicycling can actually start earlier. I'm teaching my 4 year old and 7 year old at the same time. One of our best outings is biking in the park. I put their bikes in the back of the Suburban and drive us all to the park. We unload and walk their bikes into the park.

They both have training wheels on the bikes, so I walk the entire time. I try to catch them before they fall or ride into the creek.

After the first half hour, they become comfortable. At this point, I pick a safe, level place and occasionally let them fall, so they learn what to do and what that feels like. As a result, they ride back three times as fast as they rode into the park, and with lots more confidence in their abilities.

Biking to a pre-teen is like a car to a teenager. It promotes a heightened sense of freedom and autonomy. It makes you feel great to be able to travel away from the confines of your own yard. The wind brushing your cheeks is exhilarating.

Your daughter will love it! **Create a memory that will last forever.**

25. Ages 8 to 10: *Teach her to roller-skate, bowl, and play basketball*

Your daughter's hand and eye coordination is the best it's ever been during this age period. So is her ability to balance herself. Sports, in general, become fun after about eight years old. She can have reasonable success at almost any sport now.

If she's a high energy, extrovert, then roller-skating is just the ticket for her. If she's a focused introvert, then roller-skating (because the challenge is against yourself) is also for her. It is also an activity in which the whole family can enjoy, likewise for bowling. It's good clean fun.

You can have teams if the whole family participates. Or, you can use it as quality time for talking, if just taking your teenager on a father/daughter date.

Basketball is a great "team" sport. **It's a great way to teach her about teamwork--- the whole is greater than the sum of the individual parts.** Principles of sharing, leadership, and motivation all present themselves for father/daughter discussions.

The coach for my 7 year-old's team said his wife signed him up without his knowledge. He dreaded the prospect of coaching a dozen seven-year old girls, some of whom could barely hold the ball. To his surprise, he "loved" it. (So did I.) He scheduled extra practices and arranged makeup games. We got into a rhythm of taking the girls to practice and games on Saturday mornings. The coach said he would coach again next year and even pre-register the returning girls.

26. Ages 10 to 12: *Teach her to play tennis, to COMPETE and have fun doing it*

Gordon Gekko, the character from the movie, *Wall Street*, may be ancient history, but competition is still a very important part of Western culture and civilization. **Teach your daughter to compete.**

Tiger Woods is a champion, not only because he has the most disciplined work ethnic on the tour, but more so because his father taught him to compete. Most importantly, his father taught him mental toughness, mental tenacity, and the psychology of winning.

Tennis is a great sport to teach competition. It is a sport where you are facing your competitor the entire match. You get to see his or her immediate reaction to everything you do. You learn to read his or her body language, gestures, sounds, and facial expressions.

Girls are NOT socialized to compete. It's not natural to them. Their social development focuses on relationship building and cooperating with others. Watch them socialize as children. Girls sit in groups and have endless conversations. Boys pair off and wrestle.

With encouragement and guidance, girls can compete. My oldest daughter has a shelf full of trophies (karate, basketball, tennis, and band) to prove it.

27.   Ages 12 to 14: *Teen Bible, Hymnal & Golf*

Golf, she will need it for business and socializing. It's also a game she can play for life. The fresh air and breeze will do you both a lot of good. It's another great "date" venue for your father/daughter time. Playing nine or eighteen holes together will give you lots of quality time to talk.

At 12, we gave our oldest daughter a teen Bible and a Church hymnal, both monogrammed with her name. They symbolize her movement into adolescence and womanhood. She must begin to assume responsibility for her own spirituality. **God has no grandchildren.** She must seek Him and develop a personal relationship for herself.

At fourteen, her freshman year in high school, she took her first theology course. They studied information that I only discovered in seminary: the origin of the New Testament, theories on the different writers, the books of the Catholic Bible (Apocrypha), etc. She will have her *own theology* some day, and this is a great foundation.

This is another precious time period. Somewhere between 12 and 14 years old, the "little girl" determines that Daddy doesn't understand "her" world. Yes, she becomes a *"teenager."*

Instant Messenger <u>replaces</u> Barbie!

28.   Ages 15 to 18: *More "coaching than teaching"*

I suspect. I'm close but not there yet. Stay tuned for the next book.

My theory is that kids listen intently to parents for the first fifteen years, very rarely for the next fifteen years, and then return for guidance on raising their own kids.

For now, the best advice is: "What would I do differently if she were an only child?" Try to imagine it, then work to treat her that way as often as possible.

If she <u>is</u> an only child, then try to imagine that she has siblings, and work to treat her that way once per week.

Your goal should be to develop a relationship with her that makes her want to listen ALL her life-----> your "coaching."

29.   19+: Let Her Go!
        (Yeah, Right:-)

God only knows. I'm not close to there yet!
I can wait. I'm in no hurry to get there.

Your daughter is about to leave the UFO
stage., (UFO ....Unidentified Female Object i.e.
Teenager) and embark on the greater quest of
womanhood. What ever happened to that little
girl who clung to every word her father uttered?
**Let her know that she can always come
home!** (However, that means to rest or regroup,
not freeload.)

30.   Conclusions & Reflections.

One of the best ways to raise a confident, loving, strong, God fearing daughter, is to "**love her mother passionately**." When a daughter sees this daily, she receives a vision for her own happiness and an incredible confidence in whatever Daddy has to teach her.

Due to high divorce rates and out of wedlock births, I realize this recommendation is not always achievable. However, it addresses a multitude of issues and should always be a goal.

Enjoy the journey. Raising kids is a lot of hard work. For fathers raising daughters, there's an extra dimension of stress coupled with an extra blessing of closeness and love. Enjoy your time together, whether it's on the swings in the playground, biking through the park, playing one-on-one basketball, helping with homework, or trying to get the software drivers installed for her new printer.

"A son is a son until he takes a wife. But a daughter is a daughter all of her life." Proof: After Christmas 2002, my wife and I were working diligently to pack up our family and get on the road to travel from Illinois back home to Maryland.

It was December 30th and we were trying to get back home for our Church's New Year's Eve Service. The goal was to leave as early as possible in the late morning. However, no matter what I did, my wife seemed to "dawdle" and add delays.

Her father had gone to work for the day and her mother was attending and assisting with a funeral at Church. Hence, I was surprised at how long it was taking us to get out of their home. I warned my wife that we needed to leave no later than 1 PM to avoid the Chicago rush hour traffic.

At 1 PM she was still "dawdling." At 2 PM, I was extremely antsy. At 3 PM with everything loaded in our truck, my wife began to cry. When I hugged her and asked why, she informed me that "it was still hard to say goodbye." This is after 17 years of a very happy marriage.

She was "dawdling" in the hopes of seeing her father or mother one more time to say "goodbye." **A son is a son until he takes a wife. But a daughter is a daughter all of her life."**

May God bless you in the raising of your daughter(s).

Appendix A

40 Ways Fathers Can Make a Difference

1. Give your children their spelling tests.
2. Do flash card drills to hone your children's memorization of math facts.
3. Do a science experiment with your children using Jane Hoffman's "Backyard Science" materials if other resources are not available.
4. Read your little children a story.
5. Read your bigger children the "Chronicles of Narnia" by C.S. Lewis.
6. Do the dishes with your children, while regaling them with stories of your deprived childhood in which you had to do this task without the aid of a dishwasher.
7. Do the grocery shopping.
8. Help your wife plan the school calendar and her daily schedule.
9. Take your kids to a museum or historical site.
10. Go for a hike with your children and talk about the woods, your childhood or their dreams.
11. Read your children a chapter of the Bible every evening.
12. Make sure your children read the newspaper everyday by the time they are 11 or 12.
13. Discuss current events at the dinner table. Calmly (when possible).
14. Be honest when you take them to a restaurant or

movie that charges a different rate for children under 12.

15. Read their essays and offer praise and constructive suggestions.
16. Grade their daily work.
17. Watch the children while your wife goes on a walk.
18. Read your children "Uncle Tom's Cabin."
19. Take one or two children shopping and explain to them the reasons for selecting items.
20. Take your kids to a minor-league baseball game.
21. Turn off the television.
22. Pray with your children and for them regularly.
23. Be a man and avoid exposing yourself to any pornography on television, on the Internet or in magazines.
24. Talk to your children before you impose discipline when they have done wrong.
25. Hug them afterwards.
26. Play silly games that involve lots of hugging and wrestling on the family-room rug.
27. Take your children to your childhood neighborhood and give them a tour of your memories.
28. Hug them when you leave for work and when you come home.
29. Never, ever, ever swear at your children.
30. Apologize to them when you wrong them.
31. Express genuine delight when they draw a picture for you. Put the pictures in a place that shows the children you are proud of them.
32. Plant a garden together.
33. Teach them,nicely,to strive for excellence in their work.

34. Watch your boys play baseball and your daughters perform ballet with equal enthusiasm.
35. Ask them what they want to be when they grow up.
36. Give them a vision worth living for-and worth dying for, if necessary.
37. Teach them the Pledge of Allegiance.
38. Teach them how the stock market works and give them a fantasy account using an Internet stock portfolio (like America Online's) so that they can track their earnings.
39. Tell them the percentage of your income that goes to taxes.
40. Love their mother intensely.

The author is anonymous.

Appendix B

Fathers of Daughters
1. "Daddy, I <u>need</u>......" (when really it's I <u>want</u>)
2. "Daddy, just go to the ATM and get more money!"
3. "Hoochie Mama" clothing attempts.
4. Leaving the lights on all over the house.
5. "Daddy, do I have big hips...thighs...etc.?"
6. Shopping at the mall....any mall......all malls!!!
7. Disrespect.

Daughters of Fathers
1. Dad wanting me to wear "Amish" clothes.
2. Dad not understanding a teenage girl's financial needs.
3. Dad's aversion to malls.
4. Dad wearing sweats with dress shoes------- Gross!
5. Dad's lack of interest in searching through 1,000 dresses for prom.
6. Not allowing me enough privacy.
7. Not spending enough one-on-one time together.

Appendix C

Recommended Resources

1. <u>The Bible</u>, the best selling book of all times.

2. Dan Bolin, <u>How to Be Your Daughter's Daddy: 365 Ways to Show Her You Care</u>, Pinon Press, 1993

3. <u>God's Little Instruction Book for Men</u>, Honor Books, Tulsa, OK

4. Dr. Anthony T. Evans, <u>Guiding Your Family in a Misguided World</u>, Focus on the Family Publishing, Pomona, CA, 1991

5. Website: <u>www.Fathers.com</u>

ISBN 141200129-3

9 781412 001298